THE SECRET GARDEN

By FRANCES HODGSON BURNETT

Adapted by JAMES HOWE · *Illustrated by* THOMAS B. ALLEN

Random House ⌂ New York

Library of Congress Cataloging-in-Publication Data:
Howe, James. The secret garden.
SUMMARY: An abridged adaptation of the classic story of the ten-year-old orphan who goes to live in a lonely
house on the Yorkshire moors where she discovers an invalid cousin and the mysteries of a locked garden.
[1. Orphans—Fiction. 2. Gardens—Fiction. 3. Physically handicapped—Fiction. 4. Yorkshire—Fiction]
I. Allen, Thomas B., 1928—   ill. II. Burnett, Frances Hodgson, 1849–1924. III. Title. Secret garden.
PZ7.H83727Se   1987   [Fic]   86-17788   ISBN: 0-394-86467-0 (trade); 0-394-96467-5 (lib. bdg.)

Manufactured in the United States of America   2 3 4 5 6 7 8 9 0

CONTENTS

I

MISSELTHWAITE MANOR

When Mary Lennox came to Misselthwaite Manor to live with her uncle, everyone said she was the most disagreeable-looking child ever seen. She arrived from India after an epidemic of deadly cholera had swept through that country like a hot, relentless wind. Many people had died, and among them were Mary's parents. Now, were it not for her uncle Archibald Craven, Mary would have found herself quite alone in the world.

She did not miss her parents, for she had hardly known them. Her father had always been busy. And her mother, who had not wanted a little girl at all, had handed her over to the care of servants from the time Mary was born. As she was a sickly child, all the servants obeyed her and gave her her own way in everything. And now that her parents and all her servants were gone, she fully expected that whoever took care of her next would continue to obey her and give her whatever she demanded.

Mary had a thin little face and a thin little body, thin light hair and a very sour expression. She never smiled—not once during the long voyage to England. This she made under the care of an officer's wife, who was rather glad to hand her over to the woman that Mr. Archibald Craven sent to meet her in London—his housekeeper, Mrs. Medlock.

"My word! She's a plain little piece of goods!" said Mrs. Medlock of Mary, who pretended not to hear.

"Perhaps she will improve as she grows older," the officer's wife said good-naturedly.

"She'll have to alter a good deal," answered Mrs. Medlock. "And there's nothing likely to improve children at Misselthwaite, if you ask me!"

Mary did not like the stout woman, whose face she found common and highly colored, but as she very seldom liked people, there was nothing remarkable in that.

Still, she could not help but wonder about her uncle and the place he lived in. She had heard he was a hunchback. What was a hunchback? she wondered. She had never seen one.

The next day they set out on their journey to Yorkshire. Mary sat in her corner of the railway carriage and looked plain and fretful. Her black dress made her skin look yellower than ever, and her limp hair straggled from under her black hat.

"I suppose you might as well be told something about where you're going to," said Mrs. Medlock gruffly. "It's a queer place."

Mary said nothing at all. Mrs. Medlock looked rather put out by her apparent indifference but went on.

"The house is six hundred years old and it's on the edge of the moor and there's near a hundred rooms in it, though most of them's shut up and locked. And there's a park round it and gardens and trees." She paused and took a breath. "But there's nothing else," she ended suddenly.

Mary sat still.

"What you're to be kept at Misselthwaite Manor for I don't know. *He's* not going to trouble himself about you, that's sure and certain. He never troubles himself about no one."

She stopped herself as if she had remembered something just in time.

"He's got a crooked back," she said. "That set him wrong. He was a sour young man and got no good of all his money and big place till he was married."

Mary's eyes turned toward Mrs. Medlock in spite of her intention to seem not to care.

Seeing this, the housekeeper continued. "She was a sweet, pretty thing, and he'd have walked the world over to get her a blade of grass she wanted. When she died—"

"Oh! Did she die!" Mary exclaimed, quite without meaning to. Suddenly she felt sorry for Mr. Archibald Craven.

"Yes," Mrs. Medlock answered. "And it made him queerer than ever. He cares about nobody. He won't see people. And ten to one he won't see you. Most of the time he goes away, and when he's at Misselthwaite, he shuts himself up in the West Wing."

Mary gazed out the train window at the gray rainstorm, which looked as if it would go on forever.

"You mustn't expect that there will be people to talk to you," Mrs. Medlock said. "You'll have to play alone and look after yourself."

The grayness grew heavier and heavier before Mary's eyes, and she fell asleep.

It was quite dark when she awakened.

"You have had a sleep!" Mrs. Medlock said. "We're at Thwaite Station. A carriage is waiting. We've a long drive before us."

Inside the carriage, Mary sat and looked out the window, curious to see something of the road over which she was being driven to the queer place Mrs. Medlock had spoken of. There was no knowing what might happen in a house with a hundred rooms, nearly all shut up—a house standing on the edge of a moor.

On and on they drove through the darkness, and though the rain stopped, the wind rushed by and whistled and made strange sounds. Mary felt that the wide, bleak moor was an expanse of black ocean through which she was passing on a strip of dry land.

I don't like it, she said to herself. *I don't like it,* and she pinched her thin lips tightly together.

Mary could not see the house clearly when at last they arrived, except that it was immensely long and seemed to ramble around a stone court. One window in an upstairs corner showed a dull glow.

"You are to take her to her room," a thin old man instructed Mrs. Medlock. "He doesn't want to see her. He's going to London in the morning."

And then little Mary was led up a staircase and down a long corridor and then down another and another, until finally a door was opened, and she found herself in a room with a fire and a supper on the table.

"Well, here you are!" said Mrs. Medlock. "This room and the next are where you'll live—and you must keep to them. Don't you forget that!"

It was in this way that Mary Lennox arrived at Misselthwaite Manor, and she had perhaps never felt quite so disagreeable in all her life.

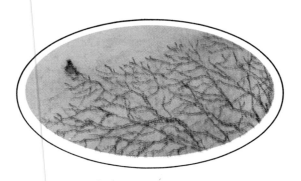

II

MARTHA

The next morning Mary was awakened by a young housemaid whose name was Martha.

"It's time for thee to get up now," said Martha in a broad Yorkshire accent. "Mrs. Medlock said I was to carry thy breakfast into the room next to this."

"Who is going to dress me?" demanded Mary.

"Cannot thou dress thyself?" Martha uttered in amazement.

"No," answered Mary quite indignantly. "I never did in my life."

"Well," said Martha, "it's time thou should learn."

It was something of a shock to Mary that the servants in Yorkshire were not in the least like the servants she had known in India. She suddenly felt horribly lonely and far away from everything she understood.

"Those are not my clothes," she said moments later, standing before the wardrobe. "Mine are black."

"Mr. Craven ordered Mrs. Medlock to get them in London," said Martha, helping Mary to button up. "He said, 'I won't have a child dressed in black wanderin' about like a lost soul. It'd make the place sadder than it is. Put color on her.' "

Secretly Mary was glad. She didn't like black things.

When she went into the next room, a good, hearty breakfast awaited her.

"I don't want it," said Mary, who had always had a very small appetite.

"Thou doesn't want thy porridge!" exclaimed Martha. "If my brothers and sisters was at this table, they'd clean it bare in five minutes."

"Why?" said Mary coldly.

"Why!" echoed Martha. "Because they scarce ever had their stomachs full in their lives. There's twelve of 'em, and my father only gets sixteen shilling a week. They're as hungry as young hawks and foxes."

"I don't know what it is to be hungry," said Mary.

"Well, it would do thee good to try it," declared the young maid.

And after Mary drank some tea and ate a little bit of toast, Martha said, "You wrap up warm, now, and run out and play."

"Will you go with me?" asked Mary.

Martha stared. "You'll go by yourself," she answered. "You'll have to learn to play like other children does. Our Dickon goes off on the moor by himself and plays for hours. That's how he made friends with the pony he now calls his own. He's got sheep on the moor that knows him and birds as come and eats out of his hand."

"Who is Dickon?" asked Mary.

"My brother, miss. He's twelve years old. Dickon's a kind lad, and animals like him."

Mary had never possessed a pet of her own and had always thought she should like one. So she began to feel a slight interest in Dickon, and as she had never before been interested in anyone but herself, it was the dawning of a healthy sentiment. It was, in fact, this mention of Dickon which made Mary decide to go out.

Martha showed her the way to the gardens. "But there's one garden is locked up," she said. "No one has been in it for ten years."

"Why?" Mary asked. Ten years was a long time. She had been born ten years ago.

"Mr. Craven had it shut when his wife died so sudden. He won't let no one go inside. It was her garden. He locked the door and dug a hole and buried the key."

Mary turned down the walk that led to the gardens. She could not help thinking about the garden that no one had been in for ten years. Here was another locked door added to the hundred in the strange house.

Mary looked about her as she walked. There were trees, and flower beds, and evergreens clipped into strange shapes, and a large pool with an old gray fountain in its midst. But the flower beds were bare and wintry, and the fountain was not playing. At the end of the path that she was following there was a wall with a door in it. The door stood open.

Inside was a garden with walls all around it, only one of several walled gardens that seemed to open into one another. Mary came upon a second door and turned its handle. She hoped the door would not open, because she wanted to be sure she had found the mysterious garden—but the door did open quite easily, and she walked through it and found herself in an orchard. Walls ran along it also. One wall, which was covered with dark green ivy, seemed to extend beyond the orchard as if it enclosed a place on the other side. Mary moved slowly along the long walk that ran beside it.

She could see the tops of trees on the other side of the wall, and when she stood still, she saw a bird with a bright red breast sitting on the topmost branch of one of them, and suddenly he burst into his winter song—almost as if he had caught sight of her and was calling to her.

She stopped and listened to him, and somehow his cheerful, friendly whistle gave her a pleased feeling. Even a disagreeable little girl may be lonely, and the big closed house and big bare moor and big bare gardens had made this one feel as if there were no one left in the world but herself. The bright-breasted little bird brought an expression to her sour face that was almost a smile. She listened to him until he flew away. She liked him and wondered if she should see him again. Perhaps he lived in the mysterious garden and knew all about it.

Perhaps it was because she had nothing whatever to do that she thought so much of the deserted garden. She was curious about it and wanted to see what it was like. Why had Mr. Archibald Craven buried the key? If he had liked his wife so much, why did he hate her garden?

She thought of the robin and of the way he seemed to sing his song at her, and as she remembered the treetop he perched on, she stopped walking rather suddenly along the path.

"I believe that tree was in the secret garden—I feel sure it was,"

she said. "There was a wall round the place, and there was no door."

That night, after Mary had finished her supper, she turned to Martha as they sat before the fire.

"Why does Mr. Craven hate the garden?" she said.

"Art thou thinking about that garden yet?" said Martha. "I knew thou would. That was just the way with me when I first heard about it."

"Why does he hate it?" Mary persisted.

"It was Mrs. Craven's garden that she had made when first they were married," answered Martha. "Him and her used to go in and stay there hours and hours, readin' and talkin' and tendin' the flowers. There was an old tree with a branch bent like a seat on it. And she made roses grow over it, and she used to sit there. But one day when she was sittin' there the branch broke, and she fell on the ground and was hurt so bad that next day she died. The doctors thought he'd go out of his mind and die too. That's why he hates it. No one's never gone in since, and he won't let anyone talk about it."

Mary did not ask any more questions. She looked at the red fire and listened to the wind howling outside the house. But as she was listening she began to hear something else. She did not know what it was, because at first she could scarcely distinguish it from the wind itself.

"Do you hear anyone crying?" she said.

Martha suddenly looked confused.

"No," she answered. "It's the wind."

"But listen," said Mary. "It's in the house—down one of those long corridors."

And at that very moment a great rushing draft blew along the passage and the door of the room they sat in was blown open with a crash, and the crying sound could be heard more plainly than ever.

"There!" said Mary. "I told you so!"

"It is the wind," said Martha stubbornly, and she ran and shut the door.

But something troubled and awkward in her manner made Mary stare very hard at her. She did not believe that Martha was speaking the truth.

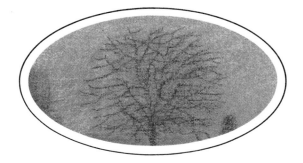

III

THE ROBIN WHO
SHOWED THE WAY

At first each day that passed was exactly like the others for Mary Lennox. Every morning she awoke and found Martha kneeling upon the hearth and building her fire, and after breakfast Mary gazed out of the window at the huge moor, which seemed to spread out on all sides and climb up to the sky. She realized that if she did not go out, she would have to stay in the big, gloomy house and do nothing—and so she went out. She did not know that this was the best thing she could have done, for when she walked or ran along the paths, she was stirring her slow blood and making herself stronger. She stayed out of doors nearly all day, and when she sat down to her supper at night, she felt hungry and drowsy and comfortable.

Mary's meals were served regularly, and Martha waited on her, but no one bothered about her in the least. Mrs. Medlock came and looked at her every day or two, but no one inquired what she did or told her what to do. Mary supposed that perhaps this was the English way of treating children.

She was even learning to dress herself, because Martha looked as though she thought Mary was silly and stupid when she wanted to have things handed to her and put on. Rather than resent Martha's familiar ways, Mary had begun to enjoy hearing about the moorland cottage, which held fourteen people who lived in four rooms and never had quite enough to eat. She was most attracted by the stories about Dickon and his animals.

"I *like* Dickon," she said to Martha one morning at breakfast. "But

I know he wouldn't like me. No one does."

"How does thou like thyself?" Martha inquired.

Mary hesitated a moment.

"Not at all, really," she answered. "But I never thought of that before."

Martha left to visit her family that day, and Mary felt lonelier than ever. She went out into the garden as quickly as possible, and the first thing she did was to run around and around the fountain flower garden ten times. When she had finished, she felt in better spirits.

"Springtime is coming," she said aloud, sniffing the air in the orchard as she walked toward the path outside the long, ivy-covered wall. Martha had told her that morning that although it was a long way off, springtime was on its way.

Suddenly she heard a chirp and a twitter, and when she looked at the bare flower bed at her left side, there was the robin she had seen during her first day in the garden. He was hopping about and pretending to peck things out of the earth. He hopped, flirted his tail, and twittered. It was as if he were talking. His red waistcoat was like satin, and he puffed his tiny breast out and was so fine and so grand and so pretty that it was as if he were showing her how important and like a human person a robin could be. Best of all, he allowed her to draw closer and closer to him.

Mary chirped and talked and coaxed, but she did not put out her hand toward him or startle him in the tiniest way. To think that he should actually let her come as near to him as that! She was so happy that she scarcely dared to breathe.

The robin hopped about under the shrubs and over to a small pile of freshly turned-up earth. He stopped to look for a worm. The earth had been turned up when a dog tried to dig up a mole and, in doing so, scratched quite a deep hole.

Mary looked at it, not really knowing why the hole was there, and as she looked she saw something almost buried in the newly turned soil. It was something like a ring of rusty iron, and when the robin flew up into a tree nearby, she put out her hand and picked up the ring. It was more than a ring, however; it was an old key, which looked as if it had been buried for a long time.

Mary Lennox stood up and looked with an almost frightened face at the key that hung from her finger.

"Perhaps it has been buried for ten years," she said in a whisper. "Perhaps it is the key to the garden!"

She looked at the key for quite a long time before putting it in her pocket and pacing up and down the walk. No one but Mary ever seemed to come here, so she could walk slowly and look at the wall or, rather, at the ivy growing on it. The ivy was a baffling thing. However carefully she looked, she could see nothing but thickly growing dark green leaves. It seemed so silly, she said to herself as she looked over the wall at the treetops inside, to be so near the secret garden and not be able to get in.

She kept the key in her pocket when she went back to the house, and she made up her mind that she would always carry it with her when she went out so that if she ever should find the hidden door, she would be ready.

The next morning, Martha returned from her home across the moor with a gift from her mother for Mary—a skipping rope. Mary, who had never seen a skipping rope before, was delighted and, once she understood what it was for, couldn't wait to run outside and try it.

She skipped around all the gardens and around the orchard, resting every few minutes. After skipping along her own special walk for a while, she stopped with a little laugh of pleasure, for there, lo and behold, was the robin, swaying on a long branch of ivy. He had followed her, and now he greeted her with a chirp.

"You showed me where the key was yesterday," she said. "You ought to show me the door today, but I don't believe you know where it is!"

The robin flew from his swinging spray of ivy onto the top of the wall, and he opened his beak and sang a loud, lovely trill. And then something wonderful happened—something that seemed to Mary to be magic.

A sudden gust of wind swung aside some loose ivy trails, and Mary jumped toward them and caught them in her hand. She had seen something underneath the ivy—a round knob that had been covered

by the leaves hanging over it. It was the knob of a door.

She put her hands under the leaves and began to pull and push them aside, her heart thumping and her hands shaking a little in her delight and excitement. The robin kept singing and twittering away as if he were as excited as she was.

She put her hand in her pocket, drew out the key, and found that it fitted the keyhole. She turned the key.

And then she took a deep breath and looked behind her up the long walk to see if anyone was coming. No one was. She held back the swinging curtain of ivy and pushed the door, which opened slowly . . . slowly.

Then she slipped through it, shut it behind her, and stood with her back against it, looking about her and breathing quite fast with excitement and wonder and delight.

She was standing *inside* the secret garden.

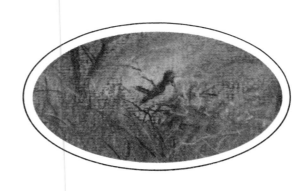

IV

THE STRANGEST HOUSE

It was the sweetest, most mysterious-looking place anyone could imagine. The high walls that shut it in were covered with the leafless stems of climbing roses, and the ground with grass of wintry brown. One of the things that made the place look strangest and loveliest was the roses that had run all over the trees and swung down long tendrils which made light, swaying curtains. Here and there they had caught at each other and made lovely bridges of themselves. It was this hazy tangle from tree to tree that made it all look so mysterious. Indeed, it was different from any other place that Mary had ever seen in her life.

She moved away from the door, stepping as softly as if she were afraid of awakening someone.

"Is it all a quite dead garden?" she said softly. "I wish it weren't." There were only gray or brown sprays and branches, and none showed any signs of even a tiny leaf bud anywhere.

But she was inside the wonderful garden, and she could come through the door under the ivy anytime. She felt as if she had found a world all her own.

The robin flew down from his treetop and hopped about or flew after her from one bush to another, as if he were showing her things. Everything was strange and silent, and she seemed to be hundreds of miles away from anyone, but somehow she did not feel lonely at all. All that troubled her was her wish that she knew whether all the roses were dead, or if perhaps some of them had lived and might put out leaves and buds as the weather got warmer.

Mary walked about for a while, stopping when she wanted to look at things. In one flower bed, she thought she saw something sticking out of the black earth—some sharp, little, pale green points.

"It *isn't* a quite dead garden," she whispered. "Even if the roses are dead, there are other things alive."

She did not know anything about gardening, but the grass seemed so thick in some of the places where the green points were pushing through that she thought they did not have enough room to grow. So she found a sharp piece of wood and knelt down and dug and rooted out the weeds and grass until she made little clear spots around them.

Mary went from place to place, digging and weeding, and enjoyed herself immensely. She worked in her garden until it was time to go in to dinner. In fact, she was rather late in remembering, and when she put on her coat and hat and picked up her skipping rope, she could not believe that she had been working for two or three hours. She had actually been happy all the time; and dozens of the tiny, pale green points were to be seen in the cleared places, looking twice as cheerful as they had looked before, when the grass and weeds had been smothering them.

"I shall come back tomorrow," she said, looking all around at her new kingdom and speaking to the trees and the rosebushes as if they heard her.

Then she ran lightly across the grass, pushed open the slow old door, and slipped through it under the ivy. She had such red cheeks and such bright eyes and ate such a hearty dinner that Martha was delighted.

After she finished eating, she went to her favorite seat on the hearth rug. Martha sat nearby.

"I wish—I wish I had a little spade," she said.

"Whatever does thou want a spade for?" asked Martha, laughing. "Art thou goin' to take to diggin'?"

Mary looked at the fire and pondered a little. She must be careful if she meant to keep her secret kingdom. She wasn't doing any harm, but if Mr. Craven found out about the open door, he would be fearfully angry and get a new key and lock it up forever.

"This is such a big, lovely place," she said slowly. "I thought that if I had a little spade and some seeds, I could dig somewhere and make a little garden."

Martha smiled. "I've just thought of somethin'," she said.

"What?" asked Mary eagerly.

"In the shop at Thwaite they sell packages of flower seeds for a penny each, and our Dickon knows which is the prettiest ones and how to make 'em grow. We could write a letter to him and ask him to go and buy the garden tools and the seeds at the same time."

Mary thought it was a wonderful idea, and Martha ran out of the room to fetch a pen and ink and some paper.

"If I have a spade," Mary whispered to herself, "I can make the earth nice and soft and dig up weeds. If I have seeds and can make flowers grow, the garden won't be dead at all—it will come alive."

Mary waited for what seemed a long time before Martha returned. Then they wrote the letter. This is what Martha dictated to Mary:

My Dear Dickon,

    Miss Mary has plenty of money and will you go to Thwaite and buy her some flower seeds and a set of garden tools to make a flower bed. Pick the prettiest ones and easy to grow. Give my love to Mother and every one of you.

Your loving sister,
Martha Sowerby

"How shall I get the things when Dickon buys them?" Mary asked.

"He'll bring 'em to you himself. He'll like to walk over this way."

"Oh!" exclaimed Mary, "then I shall see him! I never thought I should see Dickon."

And then Mary remembered something.

"Martha," she said, "when I waited so long for you to come back, I opened the door and walked down the corridor to see if you were coming. And I heard that far-off crying again, just as we heard it the other night. It couldn't have been the wind because there is no wind today."

❧❧❧

"Thou mustn't go walkin' about in corridors and listenin'," said Martha restlessly.

"I wasn't listening," said Mary. "I was just waiting for you—and I heard it. That's twice."

"My word! There's Mrs. Medlock's bell," said Martha, and she ran out of the room.

"It's the strangest house anyone ever lived in," said Mary drowsily as she dropped her head on the cushioned seat of the armchair near her. Fresh air, digging, and skipping rope had made her feel so comfortably tired that she soon fell asleep.

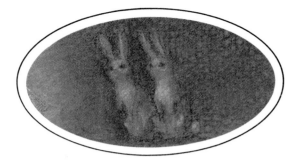

V

DICKON

The sun shone down steadily in the week that followed. Mary learned that Mr. Craven should not be returning to Misselthwaite Manor for some time, as he had gone on from London to travel in foreign lands. There would be no chance now of his discovering that she spent all her days in the secret garden, no chance of his becoming angry with her and locking up the garden forever. He would not be back until the autumn, Martha told her, and so, without telling a soul, Mary claimed the garden as her own, with no fear that Mr. Craven would take it away from her. She worked and dug and pulled up weeds, becoming more pleased with her work with every passing day.

It had been almost a month since Mary had come to Misselthwaite Manor, and she was becoming fatter and healthier—and happier— than she had ever been. She loved to be out of doors, where she felt as alive as the pale green points that sprouted all over the secret garden in the nice, clear places that Mary had made for them.

There was a laurel-hedged walk which curved around the secret garden and ended at a gate that opened into a wood. One day she thought she would skip around this walk and look into the wood and see if there were any rabbits hopping about. When she reached the little gate, she opened it and went through because she heard a low, peculiar whistling sound and wanted to find out what it was.

It was a very strange thing indeed. She quite caught her breath as she stopped to look at it. A boy was sitting under a tree, with his back against it, playing on a rough wooden pipe. He was a funny-looking

boy, about twelve. On the trunk of the tree he leaned against, a brown squirrel was clinging and watching him, and quite near him were two rabbits, sitting up and sniffing with tremulous noses—and, actually, it appeared as if they were all drawing near to watch him and listen to the strange call of his pipe.

When he saw Mary, he held up his hand and spoke to her in a low voice. "Don't thou move," he said. "It'd flight 'em."

He stopped playing his pipe and rose slowly from the ground. The squirrel scampered back up into the branches of the tree, and the rabbits dropped on all fours and hopped away, though not at all as if they were frightened.

"I'm Dickon," the boy said. "I know thou art Miss Mary. I've got the garden tools and the seeds."

He spoke to her as if he knew her quite well. But because she felt rather shy, Mary spoke to him a little stiffly.

"Will you show the seeds to me?" she asked.

They sat on a log, and Dickon began to explain the various kinds of seeds to her. She wished she could talk as he did. His speech was so quick and easy.

Suddenly he stopped and turned his head.

"Where's that robin as is callin' us?" he said.

The chirp came from a thick holly bush, bright with scarlet berries, and Mary thought she knew whose call it was.

"Is he really calling us?" she asked.

"Aye," said Dickon. "He's callin' someone he's friends with."

"I think he knows me a little," Mary said.

"Aye, he knows thee," said Dickon quietly. "And he likes thee."

"Do you think he really likes me?" cried Mary eagerly.

"He wouldn't come near thee if he didn't," answered Dickon.

"Do you understand everything birds say?"

Dickon's grin spread until he seemed all wide, red, curving mouth, and he rubbed his rough head.

"I think I do, and they think I do," he said. "I've lived on the moor with 'em so long. Sometimes I think perhaps I'm a bird, or a fox, or a rabbit, or a squirrel, or even a beetle, and I don't know it."

He laughed and began to talk about the flower seeds again. He told Mary what they looked like when they were flowers; he told her how to plant them, and watch them, and feed and water them.

"See here," he said, turning around to look at her. "I'll plant them for thee myself. Where is thy garden?"

Mary's thin hands clutched each other as they lay on her lap.

"I don't know anything about boys," she said slowly. "Could you keep a secret if I told you one? It's a great secret."

"I'm keepin' secrets all the time," Dickon answered.

Mary did not mean to put out her hand and clutch his sleeve, but she did it.

"I've stolen a garden," she said very fast. "Nobody wants it, nobody cares for it, nobody ever goes into it. Perhaps everything in it is dead already; I don't know. Nobody has any right to take it from me when I care about it and they don't. They're letting it die, all shut in by itself," she ended passionately, and she burst out crying.

Dickon's blue eyes grew rounder and rounder.

"Where is it?" he asked in a voice both curious and full of sympathy.

Mary got up from the log at once. "Come with me and I'll show you," she said.

She led him around the laurel path and to the walk where the ivy grew so thickly.

"It's this," Mary said as she stepped to the wall and lifted the hanging ivy. "It's a secret garden, and I'm the only one in the world who wants it to be alive."

They passed in together.

Dickon looked around and around about it, and around and around again.

"Eh!" he almost whispered, "it is a queer, pretty place! It's like as if a body was in a dream. I never thought I'd see it."

"Did you know about it?" asked Mary.

"Martha told me there was one garden as no one ever went inside," he answered. "Us used to wonder what it was like."

"Will there be roses?" Mary whispered. "Can you tell? I thought perhaps they were all dead."

"Eh! No! Not them—not all of 'em!" he said. "They're as wick as you or me." Mary remembered that Martha had told her that *wick* meant "alive."

"I'm glad they're wick!" she whispered fiercely. "I want them all to be wick. Let us go round the garden and count how many wick ones there are."

They went from bush to bush and from tree to tree. Dickon cut the dry and dead wood away and showed Mary how to tell when an unpromising bough or twig still had green life in it.

In no time at all they were using the new tools to dig and weed and cut away the dead wood to make room for the living.

"There'll be a fountain of roses here this summer!" Dickon proclaimed quite suddenly. And then he cried, "Why! Who did that there?" He was pointing to one of Mary's own little clearings around the pale green points.

"I did it," said Mary.

Dickon went and knelt down by them, smiling his wide smile.

"Thou did right," he said. "A gardener couldn't have told thee better. They'll grow now like Jack's beanstalk. They're crocuses and snowdrops, and these here is daffydowndillies. Eh! they will be a sight."

They worked and talked the entire afternoon, and soon they heard the big clock in the courtyard strike the hour, and it was time for Mary to go in.

"There's a lot more work to do here!" Dickon said, admiring all that they had done.

"Will you come again and help me do it?" Mary asked.

"I'll come every day if thou wants me," he answered stoutly. "It's the best fun I ever had in my life—shut in here and wakenin' up a garden."

"Dickon," Mary said, "you are as nice as Martha said you were. I like you, and you make the third person. I never thought I should like three people."

"Only three folk as thou likes?" he said. "Who is the other two?"

"Martha and the robin."

Dickon laughed. "I know thou thinks I'm a queer lad," he said, "but I think thou art the queerest little lass I ever saw."

Then Mary did a strange thing. She leaned forward and asked Dickon a question she had never dreamed of asking anyone before. And she tried to ask it in Yorkshire dialect because that was his language, and in India a native was always pleased if you knew his speech.

"Does thou like me?" she asked.

"Eh!" he answered heartily, "that I does. I likes thee wonderful, and so does the robin, I do believe!"

"That's two, then," said Mary. "That's two for me. I shall have to go now," she added mournfully. "Whatever happens, you—you never would tell about the garden—not even Martha?"

"If thou was a missel thrush and showed me where thy nest was, does thou think I'd tell anyone? Not me," he said. "Thou art as safe as a missel thrush."

And she was quite sure she was.

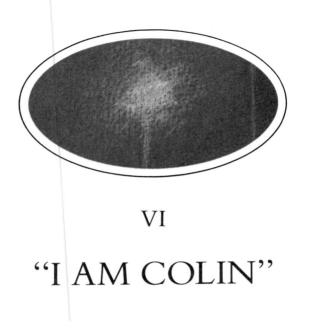

VI

"I AM COLIN"

That night Mary was awakened by the sound of rain beating against her windows and wind howling around the corners of the huge old house. The mournful sound made it impossible to fall back to sleep.

After an hour a different sound made her sit up in bed. "It isn't the wind now," she whispered. "It is that crying I heard before."

She felt that she must find out what it was. It seemed even stranger to her than the secret garden and the buried key. So she took up a candle and went out in search of the mysterious sound.

Down one long, dark corridor, then another, then yet another she went, the far-off, faint crying leading her steps all the while. The sound was becoming louder. Down this passage and then to the left, up two steps and then to the right. Suddenly she saw a glimmer of light coming from beneath a door. Someone was crying in the room beyond that door, she was sure of it, and it was quite a young someone.

She walked to the door and pushed it open. On the bed was a boy, crying fretfully. He had a sharp, delicate face that was the color of ivory. He looked like a boy who had been ill, but he was crying more as if he were tired and cross than as if he were in pain.

Mary crept nearer the boy, who turned his head on his pillow and stared at her.

"Who are you?" he asked. "Are you a ghost?"

"No," Mary answered in a whisper. "Are you one?"

He stared and stared and stared. Mary could not help noticing what strange eyes he had. They were agate gray, with black lashes all around them, and they looked too big for his face.

"No," he replied at last. "I am Colin."

"Who is Colin?"

"I am Colin Craven. Who are you?"

"I am Mary Lennox. Mr. Craven is my uncle."

"He is my father," said the boy.

"Your father!" gasped Mary. "No one ever told me he had a boy. Why didn't they?"

"For the same reason they did not tell me about you," Colin replied. "Because I should have been afraid you would see me. I don't like to have people see me or talk about me. You see, I am like this always, ill and having to lie down. If I live, I may be a hunchback. My father hates to think I may be like him. But I shan't live. Ever since I can remember, I have heard people say I am too sickly to live. At first they thought I was too little to understand and now they think I don't hear. But I do."

"Does your father come and see you?" Mary asked.

"Sometimes when I am asleep. He doesn't *want* to see me."

"Why?" Mary could not help but ask.

A sort of angry shadow passed over the boy's face.

"My mother died soon after I was born, and it makes him sad to look at me. He thinks I don't know, but I've heard people talking. He almost hates me."

"He hates the garden because she died," said Mary, half speaking to herself.

"What garden?" the boy asked.

"Oh! Just—just a garden she used to like," Mary stammered. "If you don't like people to see you, do you want me to go away?"

"No," he said, "I should be sure you were a ghost if you went. If you are real, sit down and talk with me."

And so they began to tell each other about themselves. Mary told Colin how life had been in India and how it had been since coming to Misselthwaite Manor. And Colin told her how it felt to be an invalid, shut up in a dark room with only books as companions. But one thing

stroking, but when she looked at him again, his black lashes were lying close against his cheeks, for his eyes were shut and he was fast asleep.

The moor was hidden in mist when the morning came, and the rain had not stopped pouring down. There could be no going out of doors. And so Mary spent the day with Colin in his room.

At first only Martha knew of this visit—which Mary and Colin intended to keep as secret as the garden—but then in the midst of their talking and laughing together, the door opened and in walked Mrs. Medlock and Colin's doctor.

"Good Lord!" exclaimed Mrs. Medlock.

"What is this?" said the doctor. "What does it mean?"

"This is my cousin, Mary Lennox," said Colin. "I asked her to come and talk to me. I like her. She must come whenever I send for her."

The doctor turned to Mrs. Medlock.

"Oh, sir," she panted. "I don't know how it happened. There's not a servant on the place that would dare to talk—they all have their orders."

"Nobody told her anything," said Colin. "She heard me crying and found me herself. Don't be silly, Medlock."

Mary saw that the doctor did not look pleased, but it was quite plain that he dared not oppose his patient. He felt Colin's pulse.

"I am afraid there has been too much excitement," he said. "Excitement is not good for you, my boy."

"I should be excited if she stayed away," replied Colin, his eyes flashing.

The doctor looked troubled. "But you must not forget that you tire easily," he said. "You must not forget that you are ill."

"I *want* to forget," said Colin. "She makes me forget. That is why I want her. Now go away and leave us alone."

Mrs. Medlock muttered, "Well, he does look rather better." And they withdrew.

Colin turned to find Mary gazing at him as if he had set her wondering.

"Why do you look at me like that?" he asked her.

"I was thinking," said Mary, "how different you are from Dickon."

"Who is Dickon?" he asked. "What a queer name."

"He is Martha's brother, and he is not like anyone else in the world," she began. Colin listened intently as Mary told him about the music Dickon played on his pipe and the way the animals drew near. He lay back on his cushions, and his gray eyes grew larger and larger as she talked about the cottage across the moor where fourteen people lived in four rooms. And it was all so alive that Mary talked more than she had ever talked before—and Colin both talked and listened as he had never done either before. They began to laugh over nothing, as children will when they are happy together. And they laughed so loudly that in the end they were making as much noise as if they had been two ordinary, healthy, natural ten-year-old creatures—instead of a hard, little, unloving girl and a sickly boy who believed that he was going to die.

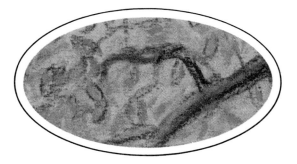

VII

NEST BUILDING

The rain continued for another week. Unable to go out, Mary spent hours of every day with Colin in his room, talking and looking at his many splendid books. Sometimes Mary read things to Colin, and sometimes he read to her. But mostly they talked.

Mary tried to be very cautious about the secret garden. She wanted to discover if Colin was the kind of boy you could tell a secret to. He was not in the least like Dickon, but he was evidently so pleased with the idea of a garden that no one knew anything about that she thought perhaps he could be trusted. Mary wondered if it might not be possible for Colin to actually visit the secret garden someday. Perhaps if he had a great deal of fresh air, and knew Dickon and the robin, and saw things growing, he might not think so much about dying.

But there had already been a change in Colin since Mary had become his friend, though she did not know it. Before, not a day would go by without his throwing a tantrum or having a fit. Now it had been a week, and he had been almost pleasant the entire time.

But what amazed Mrs. Medlock and the other servants most during this amazing week was the constant sound of laughter that burst forth from Colin's room.

On the first morning when the sky was blue again, Mary wakened very early. She opened the window, and a great waft of fresh, scented air blew in upon her.

"I can't wait!" she cried. "I am going to see the garden!"

She put on her clothes quickly and ran to the garden, and there she found Dickon kneeling on the grass, already hard at work.

"Oh, Dickon! Dickon!" she called out. "How could you get here so early! The sun has only just come up!"

"Eh!" he said, glowing. "I was up long before the sun. I couldn't have stayed away. Why, the garden was lyin' here waitin'."

The garden was full of wonders that morning—new green points pushing through the earth, swelling leaf buds on rose branches that once had seemed dead, whole clumps of crocuses burst into purple and orange and gold. And in the midst of them was a wonder more delightful than all. The robin was building a nest.

"He's like us," Dickon said in a hushed voice. "Us is near to bein' wild things ourselves. Us is nest buildin', too."

It was then that Mary told Dickon about Colin, about the midnight howling of the wind, and the far-off cries, and the small ivory-white face and the strange black-rimmed eyes.

"Them's just like his mother's eyes, only hers was always laughin', they say," said Dickon, who had known about Colin from Martha. "They say Mr. Craven can't bear to see him when he's awake, because his eyes is so like his mother's."

"Do you think he wants to die?" whispered Mary.

"No, but he wishes he'd never been born. Mother says that them is not wanted scarce ever thrives. His father would like to forget he's on earth. For one thing, he's afraid he'll look at him someday and find he's growed hunchback."

"Colin's so afraid of it himself that he won't sit up," said Mary.

"If he was out here," Dickon said, "he wouldn't be watchin' for lumps to grow on his back; he'd be watchin' for buds to break on the rosebushes, and he'd likely be healthier."

Mary agreed. "I wonder if we could bring him out here without anyone seeing us," she said.

"Us'll have him out here sometime for sure," said Dickon stoutly. "I could push his carriage well enough. He could lie out under the trees."

"He'd be like us then," Mary said.

"Aye," said Dickon, "two lads and a lass just lookin' on at the springtime, watchin' a garden grow."

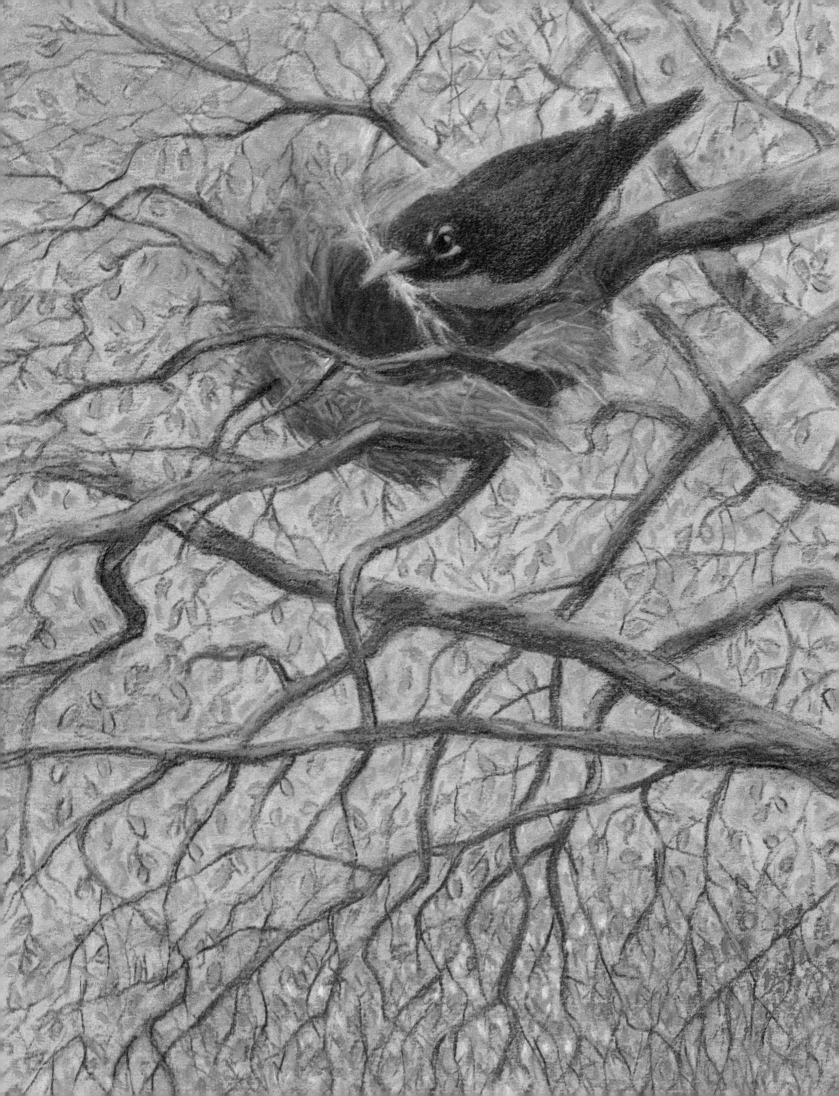

They found a great deal to do that morning, and Mary was late in returning to the house. She was also in such a hurry to get back to her work that she quite forgot Colin until the last moment.

"Tell Colin that I can't come and see him yet," she said to Martha. "I'm very busy."

Martha looked rather frightened.

"Eh! Miss Mary," she said, "it may make him angry when I tell him that."

But Mary was not as afraid of him as other people were. "I can't stay," she answered. "Dickon's waiting for me." And she ran away.

When she returned late that afternoon, she found Colin lying flat on his back in bed. Mary marched up to him, her lips pinched tightly together.

"Why didn't you get up?" she demanded.

"I did get up this morning when I thought you were coming," he answered without looking at her. "I made them put me back in bed this afternoon. My back ached and my head ached and I was tired. Why didn't you come?"

"I was with Dickon," said Mary.

Colin frowned. "I won't let you see that boy if you go and stay with him instead of coming to talk to me," he said.

Mary had no patience with Colin's sulking. "If you send Dickon away, I'll never come into this room again!" she retorted.

"You'll have to if I want you," said Colin.

"I won't!" said Mary.

"I'll make you," said Colin. "They shall drag you in."

Then great angry words flew between them. Each accused the other of being most selfish.

"I'm not as selfish as you, because I'm always ill, and I'm sure there is a lump coming on my back," said Colin. "And I am going to die, besides."

"You're not!" contradicted Mary unsympathetically.

He opened his eyes quite wide with indignation. He had never heard such a thing said before.

"I'm not?" he cried. "I am! You know I am! Everybody says so."

"I don't believe it!" said Mary sourly.

In spite of his invalid back, Colin sat up in bed in quite a healthy rage.

"Get out of the room!" he shouted, and he caught hold of his pillow and threw it at her.

"I'm going!" she said. "And I won't come back!"

That night Mary was awakened by the most dreadful noises. Colin was having a tantrum.

"I felt the lump—I felt it," he choked out when Mary entered his room. "I knew I should. I shall have a hunch on my back and then I shall die." And he turned on his face and sobbed and sobbed.

"Stop it!" Mary said fiercely. "You didn't feel a lump! All that ails you is hysterics and temper. Nurse," she commanded, "come here and show me his back this minute!"

The nurse, Mrs. Medlock, and Martha had been standing huddled together near the door, staring at her, their mouths half-open. The nurse came forward almost as if she were afraid.

"Sh-show her," Colin gasped out between two sobs. "She—she'll see then!"

It was a poor, thin back to look at when it was bared. There was just a minute's silence; even Colin tried to hold his breath while Mary looked up and down his spine.

"There's not a single lump there!" she said at last. "There's not a lump as big as a pin—except backbone lumps, and you can only feel them because you're thin. If you ever say there is a lump again, I shall laugh!"

No one but Colin himself knew what effect those crossly spoken words had on him. If he had ever had anyone to talk to about his secret terrors, if he had had childish companions and had not lain on his back in the huge closed house, he would have found out that most of his fright and illness was created by himself. And now that an angry, unsympathetic little girl insisted that he was not as ill as he thought, he actually felt as if she might be speaking the truth.

"Do you think—I could—live to grow up?" he asked.

"You probably will if you do not give way to your temper," said the nurse, "and if you stay out a great deal in the fresh air."

Weak and worn out with crying, Colin put out his hand toward

Mary, and, her own anger having passed, she met him halfway with her hand, so that it was a sort of making up.

"I'll—I'll go out with you, Mary," he said. "I shan't hate fresh air if we can find—" He remembered just in time to stop himself from saying "if we can find the secret garden," and he ended, "I shall like to go out with you if Dickon will come and push my chair."

The nurse remade the tumbled bed and straightened the pillows. Then she made Colin a cup of tea and gave a cup to Mary, who really was very glad to get it after her excitement.

"I will stay with him until he goes to sleep," Mary said to the yawning nurse. "You can go if you like."

The nurse was out of the room in a minute, and as soon as she was gone, Colin pulled Mary's hand again.

"I almost told," he said, "but I stopped myself in time. Oh, Mary! If I could get into the garden, I think I should live to grow up! Do you suppose you could tell me again what you imagine it looks like inside? I am sure it will help me go to sleep."

"Yes," answered Mary. "Shut your eyes."

He closed his eyes and lay quite still, and she held his hand and began to speak very slowly and in a very low voice.

"I think it has been left alone so long—that it has grown all into a lovely tangle. I think the roses have climbed and climbed and climbed, and now they hang from the branches and walls and creep over the ground—almost like a strange gray mist. Some of them died, but many are alive, and when the summer comes, there will be curtains and fountains of roses. I think the ground is full of daffodils and snowdrops and lilies and irises, working their way out of the dark. Now the spring has begun. Perhaps there are clusters of purple cro-cuses. Perhaps the leaves are beginning to break out, and the gray is changing, and a green veil is creeping—over everything. And the birds are coming to look at it . . . because it is . . . so safe and still. And perhaps the robin has found a mate . . . and is building a nest."

And Colin was asleep.

VIII

"I SHALL LIVE FOREVER"

Mary had her hat on when she appeared in Colin's room the next morning. He was in bed, his face painfully white.

"I'm glad you came," he said. "I ache all over because I'm so tired. Are you going somewhere?"

"I won't be long," she replied. "I'm going to Dickon, but I'll come back. Colin, it's—it's something about the garden."

"Oh! is it?" he cried out. "I dreamed about it all night. I'll lie and think about it until you come back."

In five minutes Mary was with Dickon in their garden. When she told him of the previous night's events, she could see that he felt sorrier for Colin than she did. He looked up at the sky and all about him.

"Just listen to them birds," he said. "Come springtime it seems as if all the world is callin'. And that poor lad lyin' shut up and seein' so little that he gets to thinkin' of things as sets him screamin'. Eh! we must get him out here—we must get him soaked through with sunshine. And we mustn't lose no time about it."

"Yes," agreed Mary. "When I go back to the house, I'll ask him if he would let you come to see him tomorrow morning. And then, in a bit, when there's more leaves out, we'll get him to come out to the garden, and we'll show him everything."

The garden had reached the time when every day and every night it seemed as if magicians were passing through it, drawing loveliness out of the earth and the branches with wands. It was hard to go away and leave it all, but Mary went back to the house, and when she sat down close to Colin's bed, he began to sniff the air.

"What is it you smell of?" he asked quite joyously. "It's cool and warm and sweet all at the same time."

"It's the wind from the moor," said Mary. "It's the springtime and the out-of-doors and the sunshine.

"Oh, Colin," she said. "I have something to tell you."

"What is it?" Colin held his breath.

"Dickon will come to see you tomorrow morning if you like, and he'll bring his creatures with him—the animals that he's made tame and that are his friends."

"Oh!" Colin cried out in delight.

"But that's not all," Mary went on. "The rest is better. There is a door into the garden. I found it."

"Oh, Mary!" Colin said with half a sob. "Shall I see it? Shall I *live* to get into it?"

"Of course you'll see it!" snapped Mary indignantly. "Of course you'll live to get into it! Don't be silly!"

And she was so unhysterical and natural that he came to his senses and began to laugh at himself. A few minutes afterward she was telling him not what she imagined the secret garden to be like but what it really was, and Colin's aches and tiredness were forgotten, and he was listening, enraptured.

Later that morning Colin told his doctor, "I'm going out in my chair in a day or two if it is fine. I want some fresh air."

"I thought you did not like fresh air," said the doctor.

"I don't when I am by myself," replied Colin, "but my cousin is going out with me."

"And the nurse, of course?" suggested the doctor.

"No, I will not have the nurse. A boy I know will push my carriage."

The doctor looked rather alarmed. "He must be a strong boy and a steady boy," he said. "And I must know something about him. Who is he? What is his name?"

"It's Dickon," Mary spoke up suddenly.

"Oh, Dickon," said the doctor. "If it is Dickon, you will be safe enough. He's as strong as a moor pony, is Dickon."

And so it was settled that Colin would, in a few days' time, leave his dark, musty room and go out of doors.

That night Colin slept without once awakening, and when he opened his eyes in the morning, he lay still and smiled without knowing it—smiled because he felt so curiously comfortable. It was actually nice to be awake, and he turned over and stretched his limbs luxuriously. He felt as if tight strings that had held him had loosened themselves and let him go.

Suddenly Mary burst into the room, bringing with her a waft of fresh air full of the scent of the morning.

"It has come!" she cried. "The spring has come!"

"Has it?" said Colin. "Open the window! Perhaps we may hear golden trumpets!"

Mary was at the window in a moment, and in a moment more it was opened wide, and freshness and scents and birds' songs were pouring through.

"That's fresh air," she said. "Lie on your back and draw in long breaths of it. That's what Dickon does when he's lying on the moor. He says he feels it in his veins, and it makes him strong, and he feels he could live forever and ever."

"Forever and ever! Does it make him feel like that?" said Colin, and he did as she told him, drawing in long, deep breaths, over and over again until he felt that something quite new and delightful was happening to him.

Mary was at his bedside again.

"Things are crowding up out of the earth," she ran on in a hurry. "There are flowers uncurling and buds on everything, and the rose-bushes look as wick as wick can be."

And when she paused for breath, they heard a clumping sound as if someone wearing thick, clumsy boots were walking through the long corridors outside the room.

All at once the door opened, and Martha appeared.

"Dickon and his creatures have come," she announced.

Dickon came in, smiling his nicest wide smile. A newborn lamb was in his arms, and a little red fox trotted by his side. A squirrel sat on his left shoulder, and a crow on his right, and the head and paws of

a second squirrel were peeping out of his coat pocket.

Colin sat up slowly and stared and stared. In spite of all he had heard, he had not in the least understood what this boy would be like and that his creatures would seem almost to be a part of himself. Colin had never talked to a boy in his life, and he was so overwhelmed by his own pleasure and curiosity that he did not even think of speaking.

But Dickon did not feel the least shy or awkward.

"This little fox cub is named Captain," he said, rubbing the little reddish animal's head. "And this crow here's Soot. And the squirrels, they're Nut and Shell." Then he walked over to Colin's sofa and put the newborn lamb quietly on his lap.

And then there was no wondering what to say. Questions poured forth, and Dickon answered them all. He told them how he had found the lamb just as the sun was rising three mornings ago. And as he talked, Soot flew in and out of the open window and cawed remarks about the scenery while Nut and Shell ran up and down the trunks of the big trees outside and explored their branches. Captain curled up near Dickon, who sat on the hearth rug.

They looked at pictures in gardening books, and Dickon knew all the flowers by their country names and exactly which ones were already growing in the secret garden.

"I'm going to see them!" cried Colin. "I am going to see them!"

"Aye, that thou must," said Dickon. "And thou mustn't lose no time about it."

But they were obliged to wait more than a week because first there came some very windy days, and then Colin was threatened with a cold. Almost every day, Dickon came in to talk about what was happening on the moor and in the garden.

Most absorbing, however, were the preparations to be made before Colin could be transported in secrecy to the garden. As each day passed, Colin had become more and more fixed in his feeling that the mystery surrounding the garden was one of its greatest charms. Nothing must spoil that. No one must ever suspect that they had a secret. No one must see the wheelchair and Dickon and Mary after they turned a certain corner of the shrubbery and entered the walk outside the ivied walls.

One day Colin sent for Mr. Roach, the head gardener.

"Oh, you are Roach, are you?" said Colin grandly. "I sent for you to give you some very important orders."

"Very good, sir," answered Roach, staring in amazement. The young master was neither in bed nor on his sofa. He was sitting in an armchair, and a young lamb was standing by him, shaking its tail, as Dickon knelt and gave it milk from its bottle. A squirrel was perched on Dickon's bent back, attentively nibbling a nut. The little girl from India was sitting on a big footstool, looking on.

"I am going out in my chair this afternoon," said Colin. "If the fresh air agrees with me, I may go out every day. When I go, none of the gardeners are to be anywhere near the long walk by the garden walls. I shall go out at about two o'clock, and everyone must keep away until I send word that they may go back to their work."

"Very good, sir."

"You have my permission to go, Roach," Colin said, waving his hand. "But remember, this is very important."

"Caw caw!" remarked the crow hoarsely but not impolitely.

"It's all safe now," said Colin, smiling, after the gardener had left. "And this afternoon I shall see it—this afternoon I shall be in it!"

A little before two o'clock the strongest footman in the house carried Colin downstairs and outside and put him in his wheelchair, near which Dickon waited.

As Dickon pushed the chair along, Mary walked beside it, and Colin leaned back and lifted his face to the sky. The wind swept in soft, big breaths down from the moor and was strange with a wild, clear, scented sweetness. Colin kept lifting his thin chest to draw it in.

Not a human creature was to be sighted in the paths they took. They wound in and out among the shrubbery and out and around the fountain beds, following their carefully planned route for the mere mysterious pleasure of it. But when at last they turned into the long walk by the ivied walls, the excited sense of an approaching thrill made them begin to speak in whispers.

"This is where I used to walk up and down and wonder," said Mary. "And this is where the robin flew over the wall."

"Is it?" cried Colin. "Oh! I wish he'd come again!"

"And that," said Mary with solemn delight, "is where he perched on the little heap of earth and showed me the key. And this is the ivy that the wind blew back." And she took hold of the hanging green curtain.

"Oh!" gasped Colin.

"And here is the handle, and here is the door. Dickon, push him in—push him in quickly!"

And Dickon did it with one strong, steady, splendid push.

But Colin had actually dropped back against his cushions, and he had covered his eyes with his hands until they were inside and the chair had stopped and the door was closed. Not till then did he take them away and look around and around and around as Dickon and Mary had done. And over walls and earth and trees and swinging sprays and tendrils, the fair green veil of tender little leaves had crept. Everywhere were splashes of gold and purple and white, and the trees were showing pink and snow above his head, and there were flutterings of wings and faint, sweet pipes and humming and scents and scents. And the sun fell warm upon his face, like a hand with a lovely touch. And in wonder Mary and Dickon stood and stared at him. Suddenly he looked different. A pink glow of color had actually crept all over him—ivory face and neck and hands and all.

"I shall get well! I shall get well!" he cried out. "Mary! Dickon! I shall get well. And I shall live forever and ever and ever!"

IX

MAGIC

One of the strange things about living in the world is that it is only now and then that one is quite sure one is going to live forever and ever. It was like that with Colin when he first saw and heard and felt the springtime inside the four walls of a hidden garden.

"I've seen the spring now," said Colin, "and I'm going to see the summer. I'm going to see everything grow here. I'm going to grow here myself."

"That thou will," said Dickon. "Us'll have thee walkin' about here and diggin' same as other folk afore long."

And it was indeed on that very day that Colin stood for the first time. He threw off the blanket covering his legs and gripped the arms of his chair. The strength that he usually threw into his tantrums rushed through him in a new way.

"You can do it!" Mary said over and over under her breath.

Dickon held Colin's arm, then Colin's thin legs were out, and his thin feet were on the grass. Colin was standing upright—upright!—as straight as an arrow and looking strangely tall, his head thrown back and his eyes flashing lightning.

"I can stand," he said in a new voice.

"I told thee thou could," answered Dickon.

Colin drew himself up straighter than ever. "I'm going to walk to that tree," he said, pointing to one a few feet away from him. "I can rest against it if I like. And when I want to sit down, I will sit down, but not before."

He walked to the tree, and though Dickon held his arm, he was wonderfully steady.

"Everyone thinks I'm going to die," said Colin, leaning against the tree to catch his breath. "I'm not!"

"Thou die!" Dickon said. "Nothing of the sort! Thou's got too much pluck in thee. When I seed thee put thy legs on the ground in such a hurry, I knowed thou was all right!"

And when the sun slipped over the edge and ended the strange, lovely afternoon for them, there Colin stood on his two feet— laughing.

There was magic at work in the secret garden in the months that followed. At first it seemed that green things would never cease pushing their way through the earth. Then the green things began to show buds, and the buds began to unfurl and show color, every shade of blue, every shade of purple, every tint and hue of crimson. The seeds that Dickon and Mary had planted grew as if fairies had tended them. And the roses! Rising out of the grass, tangled around the tree trunks and hanging from their branches, climbing up the walls and spreading over them, with long garlands falling in cascades—they came alive day by day.

Colin saw it all, watching each change as it took place. Every morning he was brought out, and every hour of each day when it didn't rain he spent in the garden. Even gray days pleased him. He would lie on the grass "watching things growing," he said. But when the sun was shining, Colin worked along with the others.

"I wonder what the doctor will say when he sees how strong you are becoming," said Mary one day as she watched Colin digging.

"He won't say anything," Colin answered, "because he will not be told. This is to be the biggest secret of all. No one is to know anything about it until I have grown so strong that I can walk and run like any other boy. I shall come here every day in my chair, and I shall be taken back in it. And then sometime when my father comes back to Misselthwaite, I shall walk into his study and say 'Here I am. I am quite well, and I shall live to be a man.' "

Colin had made himself believe that he was going to get well. And the thought that stimulated him more than any other was this imagining what his father would look like when he saw that he had a son who was as straight and strong as other fathers' sons.

Each day he did grow stronger, and each day he could walk more steadily and cover more ground. One morning Dickon showed him some exercises he had learned. Colin watched them with widening eyes. He could do a few while he was sitting down. Soon he did a few gently while he stood upon his feet. Mary began to do them also. From that time on, the exercises became a part of each day.

At first the robin watched Mary and Colin anxiously, worried that their strange movements might mean that they were preparing to pounce, as cats do. But then he remembered that when he himself had been made to learn to fly by his parents, he had done much the same sort of thing. He had taken short flights of a few yards and then had been obliged to rest. So it occurred to him that this boy was learning to fly—or, rather, to walk. And it seemed to be no time at all before the boy, who had once looked so frail and awkward, was walking and running about just like his two companions.

"Mary! Dickon!" Colin cried out one afternoon. "Just look at me!"

Dropping his trowel, he stood upright and stretched himself to his tallest height. Color glowed in his face, and his eyes widened with joyfulness. Mary and Dickon stopped their weeding and looked at him.

"Do you remember that first afternoon you brought me in here?" he asked.

Dickon was looking at him very hard.

"Aye, that we do," he answered.

Mary looked hard, too, but she said nothing.

"Just this minute," said Colin, "all at once I remembered it myself—when I looked at my hand digging with the trowel—and I had to stand up on my feet to see if it was real. And it *is* real! I'm *well*—I'm *well*!"

"Aye, that thou art!" said Dickon.

"I'm well!" said Colin again. "I shall live forever and ever!"

And then his face took on quite a wistful expression. "I wish my

father would come home," he said. "I want to tell him myself. I'm always thinking about it. I wish—I wish my father could see me. And my mother—"

"Eh! lad," said Dickon softly, "thy mother's in this here very garden, I do believe. She couldn't keep out of it. And thy father, he must come back to thee—he must!"

X

IN THE GARDEN

While the secret garden was coming alive and two children were coming alive with it, there was a man wandering about the world who for ten years had kept his mind filled with dark and heartbroken thinking. He was a tall man with a drawn, unhappy face and crooked shoulders, and his name was Archibald Craven.

He traveled to the most beautiful places in Europe, though he never remained anywhere for more than a few days. He chose the quietest and remotest spots. But he was so sad and so bitter that he never took in the beauty that surrounded him.

Then one day a strange thing happened. He was in a wonderful valley in Austria, and he had been walking alone through such beauty as might have lifted any man's soul out of shadow. He had walked a long way, but it had not lifted his. At last he had felt tired and had thrown himself down to rest on a carpet of moss by a stream. The valley was very, very still.

He did not know when he fell asleep and when he began to dream; his dream was so real that he did not feel as if he were dreaming. He thought he heard someone calling. The voice seemed very far away, but he heard it as distinctly as if it had been at his very side.

"Archie!" he heard, and then again, sweeter and clearer than before, "Archie! Archie!"

"Lilias! Lilias!" he answered. "Lilias! Where are you?"

"In the garden." The voice came back like a sound from a golden flute. "In the garden!"

And then the dream ended.

When he awoke, a strange calm was upon him and something more—a lightness—as if something had changed. He was remembering the dream—the real, real dream.

In the garden! he said, wondering to himself. *In the garden! But the door is locked, and the key is buried deep.*

He looked down at the stream that ran through the rich green moss. He saw birds come and dip their heads and drink in it and then flick their wings and fly away. There was one lovely mass of blue forget-me-nots growing so close to the stream that its leaves were wet, and he found himself looking at them as he had looked at such things years ago. The valley seemed to grow quieter and quieter as he sat and stared at the bright, delicate blue of the flowers.

"I almost feel as if—I were alive," he said in a whisper, and he passed his hand over his forehead. "I will go back to Misselthwaite."

In a few days he was in Yorkshire again, and on his long railroad journey he found himself thinking of his boy as he had never thought of him in all the ten years past. During those years he had only wished to forget him. He had not meant to be a bad father, but he had not felt like a father at all. He had supplied doctors and nurses and luxuries, but he had shrunk from the mere thought of the boy and had buried himself in his own misery. He scarcely ever saw him except when he was asleep, and all he knew of him—or *thought* he knew—was that he was an invalid who demanded to be given his own way in every detail.

Perhaps I have been wrong for ten years, he said to himself. *Could it be possible that I may be able to do him good?*

As the train whirled him through mountain passes and golden plains, a sense of peace came over him which brought a sort of courage and hope with it. Instead of giving way to thoughts of the worst, he actually found that he was trying to believe in better things.

When he arrived at the manor, he called for Mrs. Medlock at once. She came to him, somewhat excited and curious and flustered.

"How is Master Colin, Medlock?" he inquired.

"Well, sir," Mrs. Medlock answered, "he's—he's different, in a manner of speaking."

"Worse?" he suggested.

"Well, you see, sir," she tried to explain, "neither the doctor nor the nurse nor me can exactly make him out."

"Where is he now?" Mr. Craven asked.

"He's in the garden, sir. These days he's always in the garden with Miss Mary and young Dickon—though not another human creature is allowed to go near for fear they'll look at him."

Mr. Craven scarcely heard her last words.

"In the garden," he said.

He turned and went out of the room. He took his way, as Mary had done, through the door in the shrubbery and among the laurels and the fountain beds. He did not walk quickly, but slowly, feeling as if he were being drawn back to the place that he had so long forsaken. He knew where the door was, even though the ivy concealed it—but he could not remember exactly where the buried key lay.

So he stopped and stood still, looking about him, and almost the moment after he had paused, he started and listened—asking himself if he were walking in a dream.

The ivy hung thick over the door, the key was buried under the shrubs, no human being had passed through that door for ten lonely years—and yet inside the garden there were sounds. They were the sounds of running, scuffling feet, chasing around and around under the trees; of the uncontrollable laughter of children trying not to be heard. What in heaven's name was he dreaming of—what did he hear?

And then the moment came when the sounds forgot to hush themselves. The feet ran faster and faster—they were nearing the garden door. There was quick, strong young breathing and a wild outbreak of laughing shouts which could not be contained—and the door in the wall was flung wide open, the sheet of ivy swinging back, and a boy burst through it at full speed and, without seeing the outsider, dashed into his arms.

He was a tall boy and a handsome one. He was glowing with life, and his running had sent splendid color leaping to his face. He threw the thick hair back from his forehead and lifted a pair of strange gray eyes that made Mr. Craven gasp for breath.

This was not what Colin had expected. He had never thought of such a meeting. And yet to come dashing out—winning a race—

perhaps it was even better. He drew himself up to his very tallest. Mary, who had been running with him and had dashed through the door, too, believed that he managed to make himself look taller than he had ever looked before.

"Father," he said, "I'm Colin. You can't believe it, can you? I scarcely can myself. I'm Colin."

Colin put out his hand and laid it on his father's arm.

Archibald Craven could not believe that this was his son, standing so tall and proud and full of life before him. His soul shook with unbelieving joy.

"Take me into the garden, my boy," he said.

And so the children took him in.

The place was a wilderness of autumn gold and purple and violet-blue and flaming scarlet. Late roses climbed and hung and clustered, and the sunshine made it look like a temple of gold. The newcomer stood silent, just as the children had when they came into its grayness. He looked around and around.

"I thought it would be dead," he said.

"I thought so, too, at first," said Mary. "But it came alive."

"It was Mary who brought it to life," Dickon said.

"And Dickon and Colin, too," insisted Mary.

"And magic," said Colin, looking with wonder first at the garden, then at the tall man who stood beside him.

Then they sat down under a tree, and Colin told his father everything.

"Now," he said at the end of his story, "it need not be a secret anymore. I am never going to get into that chair again. I shall walk back with you, Father—to the house."

When Mrs. Medlock looked out the kitchen window moments later, she threw up her hands and gave a little shriek, and every servant within hearing bolted across the servants' hall and stood looking through the window with their eyes almost starting out of their heads.

Across the lawn came the master of Misselthwaite, and he looked as many of them had never seen him. And by his side, with his head up in the air and his eyes full of laughter, walked as strongly and steadily as any boy in Yorkshire—Master Colin!

FRANCES HODGSON BURNETT was born in England in 1849. She emigrated to America when she was 16 and published her first story three years later. The money she earned from her early writing enabled her family to rise above the poverty that always threatened to overwhelm them. By the time she was 28, she had published her first adult novel, which brought her fame and wealth, but it was her children's books—*A Little Princess*, *Little Lord Fauntleroy*, and *The Secret Garden*—that have become enduring classics.

She died in 1924 on Long Island.

JAMES HOWE is the award-winning author of many children's books, including *The Hospital Book* (an American Book Award nominee), *Bunnicula*, and *When You Go To Kindergarten*. He lives in New York State.

THOMAS B. ALLEN is a well-known painter and has illustrated several books for children, including *Blackberries in the Dark* and *In Coal Country*. He is currently Hallmark Distinguished Professor in the Department of Design at the University of Kansas in Lawrence.